Better
Stronger
Wiser

30 Inspirational Stories and Devotionals
for Women with Scripture Coloring Pages

Suzanne Provagna

www.Christ-centeredwellness.com

Better, Stronger, Wiser: 30 Inspirational Stories and Devotionals for Women with Scripture Coloring Pages

© 2021 by Suzanne Provagna. All rights reserved. No other part of this book may be reproduced in any form or by any electronic or mechanical means without permission in writing from the publisher, except by a reviewer, who may quote brief passages in a review.

ISBN 979-8-9851458-0-9 (softcover)
ISBN 979-8-9851458-1-6 (ebook)

Unless otherwise noted, Scripture passages are from the Holy Bible, New International Version ®, NIV® Copyright © 1973,1978, 1984, 2011 by Biblica Inc. ® Used by permission. All rights reserved worldwide.

Scriptures marked HCSB are taken from the Holman Christian Standard Bible (HCSB): Scripture taken from the Holman Christian Standard Bible © 1999, 2000, 2002, 2003 by Holman Bible Publishers, Nashville Tennessee. All rights reserved.

Scriptures marked NKJV are taken from the New King James Version (NKJV): Scripture taken from the New King James Version ®. © 1982 by Thomas Nelson, Inc. Used by permission. All rights reserved.

Scriptures marked NET are taken from the New English Translation (NET)®: ©1996-2017 by Biblical Studies Press, L.L.C. All rights reserved.

Scriptures marked Berean Study Bible are taken from the Berean Study Bible ® ©2016, 2020 by Bible Hub. Used by permission. All rights reserved worldwide.

Cover image from Canva.com. Used by permission.

For requests to translate this material into other languages or to use extended quotes from it, or to reproduce coloring pages, please contact suzanneprovagna@gmail.com.

To schedule Suzanne to speak at your church or conference, please contact suzanneprovagna@gmail.com.

For free resources to help you live a Christ-centered life, please visit my website at http://www.christ-centeredwellness.com.

CHRIST-CENTERED WELLNESS
Suzanne Provagna

Table of Contents

It's Not Fair 1

If Only. 5

My Plan 9

The Cost of Wisdom 13

What Is Your Mountain Made From? 19

What's So Wise About an Ant? 23

The Power of Common Sense 27

Releasing Forgiveness and Living in Freedom 31

Do You Have the Blahs? 37

I Didn't Get It 41

Using the Sword with Wisdom 45

It Is A Race 49

Uncover Understanding 53

Developing Patience 57

Use Your Head! 61

A New Plan 65

War Horse 71

Don't Waste Your Time 75

I Give You My Heart 79

Listen 83

I Hate It When It Hurts! 87

It's Not Easy 89

Take Care of Yourself 93

Humility is Key 99

Faceless Facebook Fraught with Problems 103

There's a Price 107

Lead Well . . . Follow Well 111

I've Got You 115

Listen to Learn 119

A Nourished Soul 123

It's Not Fair

The proverbs of Solomon son of David, king of Israel:
for gaining wisdom and instruction; for understanding words of
insight; for receiving instruction in prudent behavior,
doing what is right and just and fair.
Proverbs 1:1–3

It has always amazed me how young children and even puppy dogs have an innate sense of "fairness". Even at a young age, we understand that life should be fair. When we see that life is anything but fair, our hearts are broken. It is our broken heart that God so desires for us to give to Him. By placing this precious, personal part of ourselves into God's hands, He is able to give us the knowledge that although life is not fair on earth, His promise for everlasting life with Him will gloriously balance our sense of "fairness." When we are in heaven, it won't be "fair" that life is so beautiful, peaceful, and delightful. Heaven is the miraculous counterbalance to life here on earth.

But until we see the face of Jesus in heaven, we have kingdom work to do on earth and we must navigate through much that is unfair. This requires wisdom.

We desire to do what is right and just and fair in our kingdom work, our relationships, and in our decision-making. Proverbs 1:1–3 gives us a no-nonsense outline of how to accomplish this quest. It says the purpose of Proverbs is to gain wisdom and instruction, to understand words of insight, to receive instruction in prudent behavior, so that we are better equipped to do what is right and just and fair. The word *prudent* can be defined as: careful, economical, not wasteful. When we have careful, economical, and non-wasteful behavior, then we can obtain the cherished character quality of self-discipline.

By pursuing wisdom through reading and studying proverbs, we will learn self-discipline.

These two things I know: Life is hard. God is good. Having lost my daughter when she was only twenty-two years old is incredibly hard and still, God is good. He created a spacious place for me to stand and held me up through severe agony.

It wasn't fair to me that she died so young. It broke my heart . . . again. God took my broken heart, and because of His love and faithfulness, gave me peace, direction, solace, and love when I turned to Him. This is His promise to all of us. He will never leave or forsake us. Our God desires our hearts and our faith. He will take care of the pain and chaos left in the quake of tragedy. God is always good.

Lord God Almighty, I know that life is not fair here on earth and that it is often excruciatingly painful. You never promised that it would be easy to serve You. You told us that it would be difficult to follow You. I know Lord, that through studying Your word and specifically Proverbs, You shape us to be wiser, stronger, and better. Because we meditate on Your Word, we will be better equipped and have more experience in giving You our faith so that we survive the next storm. Until we see the light of Your Face, we thank you, El Shaddai, Lord God Almighty.

Thoughts — Prayers — Doodles

The Proverbs of Solomon son of David, king of Israel: for attaining wisdom and discipline; for understanding words of insight; for acquiring a disciplined and prudent life, doing what is right and just and fair...

Proverbs 1:1-3

If Only...

*My son, if you accept my words and store up my commands
within you, turning your ear to wisdom
and applying your heart to understanding — indeed, if you call out
for insight and cry aloud for understanding,
and if you look for it as for silver and search for it as for hidden
treasure, then you will understand the fear of the Lord
and find the knowledge of God.
For the Lord gives wisdom;
and from His mouth come knowledge and understanding.
Proverbs 2:1–6*

We have a baby monitor that allows us to see and hear our son when he is sleeping. When he awakens from his nap, he often plays for a few minutes in his crib. It is when he cries out, "Mom" that I come to him. If he wants me, he will cry out and search for me, and I will always come to him.

If we want wisdom, we must cry out and search for it. God will always come to us and point us in the right direction. He sees us and cares for us deeply. Sometimes he lets us "play in our cribs" a little while, and we may get frustrated because His timing is not exactly as we would like. His timing often puzzles me, but maybe He wants us to think harder about our situations. Maybe He wants us to take more or less responsibility for where we are or what we have said. This I know for certain: His Scripture is truth and memorizing His Word and being able to speak it aloud helps us to be shaped by the Holy Spirit.

Never miss the fact that this proverb begins with ownership. We *belong* to God. We are sons and daughters of the Creator of the Universe, the Maker of All. We are sons and daughters of the One True God, El Shaddai, the Lord God

Almighty. God is our Father and we are His. He cares about every part of our lives.

Do we accept His words? Do we believe His words are true and powerful? Do we believe, as John 1:1 states, "In the beginning was the Word and the Word was with God and the Word was God"?

If we store up His commands by memorizing His Word, being interested in learning wisdom, asking God to show us understanding, and literally calling aloud for insight and understanding and if we search for it as for a hidden treasure, *then* God will give us wisdom and knowledge and understanding.

Dear Father God, I am so thankful that you call us Your sons and daughters and that we are part of Your family. You desire for us to make wise choices. We accept Your Word and desire to store it in our hearts that You may guide, teach, reprove, and encourage us to be more like You. Right now, we cry out to You to give us wisdom in all of our interactions today. In all that we say and do let us honor You, Father. Help us Lord, to put Your Word in front of our eyes many, many times during our day so that we commit it to memory and store up Your commands as Your Word teaches. And thank you, God, that You see fit to give us Your wisdom. Amen.

Thoughts – Insights – Doodles

My Plan

Trust in the LORD with all of your heart and lean not on your own understanding; in all your ways submit to him, and he will make your paths straight.
Proverbs 3:5–6

It cracks me up how hard it is for me to trust in the Lord with all of my heart and lean not on my own understanding. It seriously makes me want to "guffaw"!

I like the idea of controlling where I'm headed in life and what my life should look like. I have it planned. I have almost always had a plan. And yet, my life barely resembles what I planned. Some things have been better than I could have imagined and some things have been much more difficult and painful than I could have imagined—and I know I didn't plan that.

I have had this verse memorized for a couple of decades and it still challenges the daylights out of me. This is my best internalization of it at this moment in my life:

Trusting in the Lord with ALL of my heart is a leap. It is an act of faith and it comes from a place of feeling secure with the One to whom I give my heart. I willfully at this moment give ALL of my heart to Jesus Christ and ask Him to fill me up with His love. With all of my heart given to Jesus, I want what He wants above what I want. I desire to please Him more than pleasing myself. Since I'm a selfish person by birth, this is an act of supernatural means which is made possible when I meditate on His law day and night.

I am not perfectly comfortable leaning on my own understanding. I have seen where that can lead me and it's not always pretty. When I take away what I have "leaned on" and instead replace it with a sensitivity to the Holy Spirit and a working practice of obeying the Holy Spirit, then my every day, often mundane- like life, becomes extraordinary, even on days when I do not venture outside the walls of my home. When I acknowledge the Holy Spirit in ALL of my ways, He directs my path. He directs my every-day walk through life and *that* is exciting and filled with possibilities. It is a purposeful life . . . it is a purposeful walk. Whether you are serving in a church, another country, in your workspace, or in your family—trusting in the LORD with ALL of your heart changes your everyday path into one that is supernaturally created. This is a journey that will change your life and others' lives to reflect the love and purpose of God our Father.

Lord Jesus, you know that I am a weak and selfish person and that is not easy for me to say. I want to be filled with Your love, Your grace, Your justice, and Your mercy. I want to serve You and trust You with ALL of my heart. Please help me turn to You in prayer and through memorizing Your Word, and through worshiping You in song so that my heart can stay focused on You. I love you Jesus with ALL of my heart and I trust in You over and above and beyond my own understanding. Help me to walk through this day being sensitive moment by moment to Your Holy Spirit. Help me to obey You immediately so that You can use me to further Your Kingdom. Thank you and Amen.

Thoughts — Prayers — Doodles

The Cost of Wisdom

He also taught me, and said to me:
"Let your heart retain my words;
Keep my commands, and live.
Get wisdom! Get understanding!
Do not forget, nor turn away from the words of my mouth.
Do not forsake her, and she will preserve you;
Love her, and she will keep you.
Wisdom is the principal thing;
Therefore, get wisdom.
And in all your getting, get understanding.
Exalt her, and she will promote you;
She will bring you honor, when you embrace her,.
She will place on your head an ornament of grace;
A crown of glory she will deliver to you."
Proverbs 4:4–9 (NKJV)

A few years ago, I found myself eating healthy foods, taking care of myself, being centered with Christ, and feeling at peace with my life. Then my environment changed. I was around a very toxic person and realized that I had begun mindlessly overeating. It was not honoring to God or to myself, and I wasn't happy about it. I stubbornly decided not to run away from the reasons that I wanted to overeat. I kept asking, "Why?" even though it was emotionally and intellectually draining. It took discipline, perseverance, and time to get down to the very root of my feelings and uncover truth. It was worth every bit of effort.

Jesus told parables that uncovered powerful truths to those who worked to understand Him. Our problems in life hold powerful truths when we allow the light of Jesus Christ to shine into them. There is no darkness with God. "Even the darkness will not be dark to You; the night will shine like the day, for darkness is as light to You" Psalm 139:12.

Giving our questions and feelings over to God allows Him to empower us to see situations with a healthier perspective and denies the enemy a foothold. We bring all things into the light of Jesus Christ, and the darkness must flee!

Wisdom has a cost. Good health has a cost. Foolishness has a cost. Poor health has a cost. To reveal wisdom we must find truth, which costs us effort and discipline. It requires discarding frivolity and is often a painful undertaking. This is also a cost. We are no longer able to bury our heads in the sand and declare "all is right" when, in truth, it is not all right. Seeking wisdom is a deliberate action. It is not for the faint of heart. It takes courage and is often uncomfortable. However, pursuing wisdom is imperative to becoming a mature Christian.

Another day I found myself busier beyond busy, dealing with a lot of changes, and around the same toxic person, but I kept God's Word front and center in my mind. I had my water and herbal tea and had such peace about my life. This is the "me" that I desire to become stronger and this is the "me" that is closer to Christ. This is the more mature and wiser "me" who understands the value of enduring discomfort for wisdom's sake.

"Peace I leave with you; my peace I give you. I do not give to you as the world gives. Do not let your hearts be troubled and do not be afraid" (John 14:27).

Lord, help me to focus on You and Your wisdom. Help me to discipline myself to keep Your Word close to my heart and my mind so that Your peace will be in me. I know there is a cost involved to have wisdom and it is more than worth the price. For if I do not pursue wisdom, foolishness awaits me. Thank You, Lord, that all that we need is in You and that Your Word holds the wisdom we need to navigate through this world in ways that honor You. Amen.

Thoughts — Prayers — Doodles

Wisdom is the principal thing; therefore, get wisdom. Though it cost all you have, get understanding.

Proverbs 4:7

What Is Your Mountain Made From?

Let your eyes look straight ahead; fix your gaze directly before you.
Give careful thought to the paths for your feet
and be steadfast in all your ways.
Do not turn to the right or the left; keep your foot from evil.
Proverbs 4:25–27

I used to run a lot of 5k races. I trained hard by running almost every day. I discovered that if I ran with my eyes looking far ahead to the next half mile, I would lose hope, lose energy, and lose motivation. But when I looked at the next six to twelve feet in front of me, I was able to stay motivated, choose level paths and avoid the obstacles . . . like dog poop and yard toys left out and the water sprinklers that hid just below the top edges of the grass. I was able to avoid falling (most of the time).

When choosing goals—whether they are educational, spiritual, intellectual, physical, or emotional—it is wise to be crystal clear about them. Write your goals down and then break up the journey into smaller steps *and* . . . keep your eyes fixed directly before you.

Every goal I ever had looked like a mountain. Some of those mountains look like walls of rocks covered with snow and ice. Intimidating and scary . . . and I fear falling or not finishing. Climbing mountains requires the dismantling of fear.

Thankfully one of God's specialties is dismantling fear. He does this through our faith in Him; as it says in Matthew 17:20, "Faith can move mountains." Where I see snowy ice-covered rocks, God can view it as a mountain made of twigs. And when I look to the Lord for help, he takes the twig off the mountain, breaks it up and scatters it on the ground so that I can confidently put my foot down and take the next step. God empowers us to do His work with faith, not fear.

It is imperative to occasionally stop and re-access where the mountain is and what it looks like. Are our mountains made of rocks or twigs? Are we being led by faith or fear?

Wisdom says we should know our goal, plot our course, and keep our eyes on that path. "Fix your gaze directly before you." This means we are not keeping our eyes looking at the top of the mountain, for if we do this and try to walk, we will certainly fall. The only wise way to approach our mountains is to keep our eyes fixed on Jesus. He will show us where to put our next step. He will guide our every move, make our paths level, and walk before us.

Lord Jesus, You see all and You know all. You know what goals you would like for us to obtain. With Your help, we can be deliberate about our goals and keep our eyes fixed directly before us, on the power that Your Holy Spirit gives us. Father, You can keep us from swerving to the right or the left. You, Holy Spirit, will keep our feet from evil and keep us on the path to accomplishing Your work here on earth. Thank you and amen.

Thoughts — Prayers — Doodles

Give careful thought to the paths for your feet and be steadfast in all your ways.

Proverbs 4:26

What's So Wise About an Ant?

Go to the ant, you sluggard; consider its ways and be wise!
It has no commander, no overseer or ruler,
yet it stores its provisions in summer and gathers its food at harvest.
Proverbs 6:6–8

I can still picture my elderly dad in his overalls, sitting in the well-worn chair in his pole barn and reading the Wall Street Journal (usually in its entirety) while keeping himself warm by the electric heater. Dad had been a barber and a farmer. He never went to college, and he never stopped educating himself.

For as long as I can remember I have feared two character qualities . . . being stupid and being lazy. It was Dad who helped instill those fears. For him, being "stupid" meant failing to use common sense, a word that could apply to even the most educated person. But even worse than lacking common sense was a person who was lazy . . . someone who was unwilling to work. I believe Dad was trying to teach me wisdom by stressing the importance of using common sense and working hard.

The ant that is esteemed in this proverb was considered wise . . . this teeny, tiny, insect that we look down upon and maybe unceremoniously squash on the countertop . . . this pride-less, unimpressive-looking, look-a-like insect is considered wise because of its "ways". It is not wise because of how it looks, or its education, or its social-standing, or its title, or its salary—it is wise because of its "ways." The sluggard is told to look at the ant's ways and be wise.

An ant has a purpose. Its purpose is for the greater good of its colony (its people, its tribe). It does its work, step by step, and works diligently all day long. Even when there is an obstacle in its way, it will go around or above or below that roadblock and get right back on track. Sometimes it must even avoid poisonous traps!

We have definitely been given obstacles to go around when it comes to doing the work of the Kingdom. The 2020 Coronavirus is a formidable and unique obstacle. However, it is our wise duty to go around the obstacles set before us. We must put one foot in front of the other and continue our Kingdom work, not swerving to the right or the left unless there is an obstacle in front of us. When we get to the obstacle, we go around it and get back on to task immediately. We have work to do for the Kingdom. Coronavirus may have changed our titles, our salaries, or our social-positions, but because we work for the Kingdom, we have not been "laid-off." We have work to do and the God of the Universe will help us to see what that work is—when we love and seek Him with all of our heart, mind, and soul.

Lord Jesus, what do you want me to do for Your Kingdom today? Who should I ask to pray for me and who do you want me to reach out to for help? I thank you God for this unique opportunity—for such a time as this to do Your Kingdom Work. Please help me to work diligently putting one foot in front of the other, staying on task, going around obstacles and always giving glory to You my God in all things! Amen.

Thoughts — Prayers — Doodles

Go to the ant you sluggard; consider its ways and be wise!

Proverbs 6:6

The Power of Common Sense

I, wisdom, dwell together with prudence;
I possess knowledge and discretion.
Proverbs 8:12

My grandmother lived through the depression. She was a first-grade teacher, and when she died, she had saved over one hundred thousand dollars. Her home was tidy and uncluttered. She always looked nice and neat and wore dresses almost every day. When we cleaned out her closet, she only had nine dresses. She was a minimalist before it became a book or an online course. It made sense to her to live this way. She was both generous and prudent. She gave generously to her church and rewarded me and my siblings with five dollars on every major holiday if we hadn't bitten our nails! And she always seemed to have time to have a conversation with me. My grandmother was both wise and prudent.

Wisdom is common sense on steroids. Prudence is using resources wisely and wasting nothing. These two things live together. Wisdom lives with prudence; or, to say it another way, common sense lives with wasting nothing, including time.

We live in an age of excess, except for when we don't. My grandmother lived through the depression and as I'm writing this, the world is in the midst of the Coronavirus pandemic. Right now, toilet paper, milk, eggs, and other items are being rationed. They are not in excess.

Wisdom and prudence live together. To be wise, we must be prudent. We must be prudent with what we own and what we buy. Some of us have lived this way all along and some of us, not so much. Pursuing wisdom also means pursuing prudence, or wasting nothing. Sometimes wasting nothing means getting rid of "things" that you don't need or use. Things take up precious space, and it takes time to sort through things. Now might be a good time to bless someone else with some of your things.

Lord Jesus, You see all, You know all, and You love us more than we can ever imagine. What are the things in our lives that you want us to give away? Please guide us today and throughout our lives to know what, when, and where we need to be more prudent and give us the strength, discipline, and wisdom to follow through. To You, Jesus, be all glory forever and ever, Amen.

Thoughts — Prayers — Doodles

I, wisdom, dwell together with prudence; I possess knowledge and discretion.

Proverbs 8:12

Releasing Forgiveness and Living in Freedom

The wise in heart accept commands,
but a chattering fool comes to ruin.
Proverbs 10:8

Jesus commands us to forgive as He says in Mark 11:25 "And when you stand praying, if you hold anything against anyone, forgive them, so that your Father in heaven may forgive you your sins."

But what if the enemy could hold the concept of "forgiveness" hostage? We would be in such trouble! We would often feel inadequate, sad, and angry. We would see more divisiveness, arrogance, and self-righteousness. We would never attain the goals that God has for us here on earth because not forgiving allows the enemy to keep us distracted from realizing our potential.

Forgiveness is challenging whether it's forgiving others or ourselves, but it is foundational in the message and acceptance of Jesus Christ. Jesus came down to earth and died on the cross to forgive us our sins. Forgiveness is intricately interwoven into our dependence on the supernatural power of Christ in us.

The truth is that I know that I am inadequate. I am not smart enough, wise enough, or disciplined enough to do God's work (including writing this book) but the power of Christ in me is all of those things and more. With Christ in me, I can do these things and more just as it says in Philippians 4:13 "I can do all this through Him who gives me strength".

Through the very act of forgiving myself for not being enough I am able to accept the power of Christ in me to do the work that needs to be done—His work . . . His kingdom . . . His Way . . . His timing.

God forgives us for being selfish, impolite, greedy, jealous, or foolish. We need to forgive ourselves and others for doing the same. "Forgive us our sins, for we also forgive everyone who sins against us" (Luke 11:4). God created families which are held together by relationships. God didn't give me a husband, children, family, and friends so that I could sit back and be prideful, or so that they or I would be perfect and wonderful. He gave us relationships so that through the difficulties we could learn to trust Him more, learn to be shaped by Him, and learn to love better. I ask God to arrest my pride that I may rest in Jesus Christ. He can and will take care of all details as I trust in Him.

It is wise to forgive. It is a prudent use of your time, your heart, and your mind. It is foolish to think that hanging onto anger, jealousy, greed, selfishness, or rudeness will serve us better. Of course, those feelings may be completely justified for some reason but what I am saying and reminding myself of is this: Jesus Christ took on all of our sins . . . every one of yours and mine and all people before and after us. Jesus Christ took on the pain, the suffering, the separation from God for all of our sins. We owe it to Him to forgive ourselves and others. We owe Jesus Christ our trust. He has earned it by completing the most difficult task ever set before anyone here on earth. As we work through the difficult memories, and events, and things we have lived through in this lifetime, let us remember that He suffered more. And all of His suffering He did voluntarily that we could be forgiven. What power! What love! What forgiveness!

Lord Jesus, the ability to forgive is not something that I do easily. I confess to being prideful, arrogant, and self-righteous. I ask You, Jesus, to give me a humble heart that I may know Your power in me. I ask You, Jesus, to give me a forgiving heart that I may do Your kingdom work with passion, perseverance, and clarity. Thank you, Lord, even that forgiveness is difficult for it reminds me to rely on Your supernatural power in me. Please help me to serve You with a humble and forgiving heart today. Amen.

Thoughts — Prayers — Doodles

Do You Have the Blahs?

When there are many words, sin is unavoidable,
But the one who controls his lips is wise.
Proverbs 10:19 (HCSB)

I met a person in ministry who talked too much. In a conversation at least ninety percent of it was spent with her speaking. Although she had great integrity and moral character it was very difficult to feel "understood" and the church had a difficult time growing. I don't remember her words crossing over into gossip, or anything inappropriately shared, but great leaders must be great listeners. Wise leaders are wise listeners.

Sometimes talking too much comes from nervousness. Maybe we become uncomfortable with silence and words start to spill out to fill the void. Most of us have been guilty of this at one time or another. But we can't stuff those words back into our mouths no matter how fast or hard we try. It is wiser to hold our tongues.

My dad didn't talk a lot. I remember having lunch with him one day. I was nervous beforehand because the silences could be awkward for me. I decided that I would endure the silences and not interpret them to mean anything more than what they were—moments of silence. That's okay. "Be still, and know that I am God" (Psalm 46:10). If I'm going to learn to listen well to others or to the Holy Spirit, then I must learn to be quiet and endure moments of silence.

Thankfully, it is more interesting to speak less. I know what is in my mind, but I don't know what is in another person's mind. Listening well gives me information, understanding, and discernment.

Communication is necessary for good relationships. It is not one-sided. We speak and we listen. This process begins the moment we are born. As adults, we expend much energy and time helping children learn to speak but very little time helping them learn to listen well. Lucky for us, we can change the balance right now by memorizing Proverbs 10:19 and putting it into action. Listening well makes every single day an exciting challenge.

Lord Jesus, You never close your ears to us. You promise to listen and to always be here for us. Thank you. Please help us to become excellent listeners and communicators, so that we can successfully share the love and knowledge of Jesus Christ to one and all. Amen.

Thoughts — Prayers — Doodles

When words are many
sin is not absent,

But
he who holds his tongue
is wise.

Proverbs 10:19

I Didn't Get It . . .

*Fools show their annoyance at once,
but the prudent overlook an insult.
Proverbs 12:16*

There were ten volunteer men and women seated around the three tables. We were facing each other and taking turns reporting on the tasks we had finished on behalf of the professional organization. As one lady, who helped her husband run a business and had two young children at home, gave her report, she was rudely interrupted by the president, who proceeded to criticize her actions. My mouth dropped. I looked at her with the expectation that she would let him have it. She did not let him have it, and I didn't get it. Instead, she listened and asked him questions. She ended the exchange by asking him what he would prefer her to do. She then quickly said she would do that.

Wisdom from Proverbs says if we're prudent (using our time and energy wisely), then instead of showing we're annoyed right away with what we perceive to be an insult, we may overlook it, or look over it. If we looked over, what would we be looking over to? When you're traveling, sometimes you'll see a sign that says "overlook" ahead. It always has a view straight down and a view across the way—looking over the divide. We could choose to only look down and we would miss the beauty that is just across the way. Jesus wants us to keep our eyes on Him and on what is "across the way"—our eternal home in heaven.

Jesus Christ honors relationships. He showed us this firsthand by choosing His disciples. They were His best friends and He lived and worked with them. He must have been constantly overlooking annoyances. I mean, this is God . . . living with man! What was He looking over to? He had and always has our best interest at heart. Jesus wants us to become more like Him — more loving, wiser, stronger, better. Isn't that what we want for ourselves and for those we love?

When the lady in the meeting refused to show annoyance, she showed wisdom. She looked over the annoyance and fixed her eyes on what was important, which was doing the work that the president prioritized. She listened and asked questions. I reached out to her after the meeting and in just a few minutes learned that she was a strong Christian. At the time, I did not have a personal relationship with Jesus Christ. Seeing her actions elevated my curiosity in Christianity and made an immediate impact. Now, "I get it."

Lord, Jesus, today when someone annoys me, help me to pause and look past the divide and over to the view across the way—the one where You, Jesus are longing to mold and form me. I pray that when I annoy someone today, that he gives me grace and overlooks my insensitivity. Help me, Jesus, to look past insults and to see the bigger picture that You have painted. Help me Father to always take time to look for ways to have conversations with unbelievers. May You be glorified in all that I say and do today. Amen.

Thoughts — Prayers — Doodles

Using the Sword with Wisdom

*The words of the reckless pierce like swords,
but the tongue of the wise brings healing.
Proverbs 12:18*

Reckless is a word used to describe teenagers who act as though they can't get hurt or they can't hurt others. Reckless can describe a teenager's behavior when they don't give much thought before doing something. Being reckless can lead to wrecks. Reckless behavior can lead to choices that have no easy outcomes, or to choices that will make life difficult forever, or even to choices that lead to death—that is reckless behavior.

We may not consider our own behavior to be reckless, but our words and how we speak may be reckless at times. Reckless words pierce like a sword. A sword can cut deeply or make a scratch, but it always leaves a mark and sometimes it leaves a permanent scar. The same is true of our words. If our words are reckless, they can make a scratch or cut deeply enough to cause a permanent scar.

What would our day look like if we thought about our words as being that powerful? Powerful enough to make a scratch or a permanent scar? I think we'd keep our sword in the sheath most of the time. We'd keep our words in our heads most (or at least more) of the time. Would a day be so bad if we kept most of our words in our head? Maybe we should it try it today . . . and tomorrow . . . and the next day. Maybe sitting with the truth that our words are *that powerful* will help us to focus on the last part of the Proverb: "but the tongue of the wise brings healing." That is a beautiful truth. We can pour out healing to others when we are wise. We become wise by pursuing the Wisdom of God, by studying Proverbs, by meditating on His Word, by walking with the wise, and by praying for wisdom.

Lord Jesus, help me to memorize Your Word, and specifically Proverb 12:18. "The words of the reckless pierce like swords, but the tongue of the wise brings healing." It is my hope to heal people and not wound them. Jesus, it is my desire to please You and Your Word says that You promise wisdom to all who seek it through Your Holy Bible. I thank you that I am able to be Your servant today. Help me to keep my heart open to hearing from You and my mind on Your Words. Amen.

Thoughts — Prayers — Doodles

The WORDS of the Reckless Pierce like a  sword but the tongue of the wise brings healing.

Proverbs 12:18

It Is A Race

*He who walks with wise men will be wise,
But the companion of fools will suffer harm.
Proverbs 13:20*

I have a trophy on my dresser. I got it for winning a 5K running race, but that isn't why it's there. It reminds me that I was able to do something that I was scared to death to do. It represents my decision to willfully put myself in uncomfortable situations in order to learn from wiser, better-trained comrades.

Entering the race put me far outside of my comfort zone, and on race day it took all of my courage to follow through. I set the alarm for 5:30 a.m. and drove for an hour in the snow, ice, and dark to a place I'd never been before. After finding the starting venue, I walked into a room and found myself noisily surrounded by nearly two hundred people of which I knew none. There were long tables and long lines, and everyone seemed to know what to do.

"Do you have your chip?" a lady from behind a table asked me. "No", I replied, "What's a chip?" I learned that a chip gets tied onto your shoelace and when you step onto a mat at the beginning and end of the race it records your time. Good to know. New information. New people. New rules. A big part of me doesn't like new things. I enjoy routines.

But I will never know what I don't know if I don't do new things. Intentionally seeking out people who are really good at what they do is wise. Intentionally seeking out great runners will make me a better runner. Seeking out wise people will make me wiser.

What if we really acted like life was a contest and there was a prize at the end? How would we be training? Who would be training with us? What would we need to learn in order to win? Paul says in Philippians 3:14 "I press on to reach the end of the race and receive the heavenly prize for which God, through Jesus Christ, is calling us" (NLT).

When in a competition—whether it's running a 5K, a business, or something else—we become better when we train with others who know more than us. In this competition of life, we become wiser when we walk with the wise. Being wise helps us to win souls for Christ. Being wise protects us and trains us to live a life of discipline, knowledge, and discernment.

Intentionally seeking out wise brothers and sisters in Christ is an effort that benefits us *and* the kingdom of God. Walking with the wise trains us harder, faster, and better. It strengthens our effectiveness to accomplish Kingdom work.

We find wise people in our families, neighborhoods, churches, books, podcasts, radio programs, and the Bible. Being around wise people keeps us on our toes, and reading about wise people broadens our understanding of life experiences.

The proverb states: "but a companion of fools suffers harm." Wisdom protects. Foolishness harms. We are all foolish at times, but Scripture says that if we seek wisdom from God, He will give it to us. This is the difference between the wise and the foolish. The wise are set apart because they continue to seek wisdom from God and the foolish do not.

Lord God, by wisdom You created the heavens and the earth. You value wisdom and You value us. Please help us to seek wise brothers and sisters as we run this race on earth. We desire the prize at the end of this lifetime to hear the words, "Well done, good and faithful servant. Enter into the Kingdom of God." Thank you, Father. Help us to serve You well today and always. Amen.

He who walks with wise men will be wise, but a companion of fools suffers harm.

Proverbs 13:20

Uncover Understanding

*Those who disregard discipline despise themselves,
but the one who heeds correction gains understanding.
Proverbs 15:32*

I dreamt I was in the green room of the recital hall with the orchestra ready, conductor waiting, audience sitting in anticipation . . . and I did not have my concerto memorized. I was trying to act like I had it together but inside my mind it was more chaotic than I could understand. I knew I was going to fail miserably. Then morning comes and instead of stepping onto the stage I step into my life.

Every time I have this dream it gives me the opportunity (maybe even responsibility) to look at my life and dissect where and why I have anxiety. I believe that discipline decimates anxiety.

In reality, almost forty years ago I walked onto a stage and played a difficult concerto with a demanding conductor and a full house. I was confident, completely prepared, and the performance went very well. Every note was etched into my memory so deeply that even now many of them are still visible in my mind's eye. This is because I was committed to the discipline of practicing the piano hours upon hours, days upon days, and years upon years.

If I had disregarded or ignored this discipline of daily practice, then I would have despised myself—for I would have missed an awesome opportunity to win the competition and the enjoyment of performing as a solo pianist with an orchestra.

Discipline can come from inside us in the form of self-discipline (daily habits) or it can come from others in the form of correction. Not every discipline is merited, but all discipline deserves thought and evaluation.

God disciplines those He loves. Trusting that God disciplines us *because* He loves us is key. Knowing that self-discipline is integral in the development of a mature Christian encourages us to be more deliberate about what habits we choose to practice in our daily lives.

Lord Jesus, You came down from heaven as God and lived a perfect human life. You were completely human and completely God. You felt anxiety. You practiced self-discipline. You listened and evaluated others' corrections. You kept the Word of God firmly in Your mind. You were always ready to know what to say and what to do. We are mere humans on this earth, here today and gone tomorrow. Help us Jesus, to live a life with healthy self-discipline, through the power of Your Holy Spirit. Help us Jesus, to discern the merit of others' corrections. Help us to listen so very closely to the Holy Spirit so that we have the understanding that You desire for us as we walk through this life and into eternity with You. Amen.

Thoughts — Prayers — Doodles

Those who disregard discipline despise themselves, but the one who heeds correction gains understanding.

Proverbs 15:32

Developing Patience

A man's wisdom yields patience;
it is to one's glory to overlook an offense.
Proverbs 19:11

When I was about twelve years old my mother thought it was time for me to learn to sew a shirt. She was and still is an amazing seamstress and taught all four of her daughters to sew. My assignment was to sew a shirt with long sleeves and a collar. I looked at the picture on the pattern and decided that sewing a shirt would be fun. I set to work with a good attitude and a positive mindset . . . which lasted for about an hour. I endured working on that shirt for what seemed like days on end. Sewing—ripping out, sewing—ripping out, repeating this process over and over and over again.

I knew mom would not let me give up on finishing that shirt, so I did what any impatient child might do. I deliberately cut through the collar and enough fabric that it was no longer salvageable. The project was done!

When God knit me together, He gave me more passion than patience. This has seriously, often brought me to my knees. Thankfully, patience can be acquired through the pursuit of wisdom. When we set our minds on pursuing wisdom we will develop invaluable character qualities, such as patience.

Understandably, some offenses should not be overlooked but must be addressed. Wisdom gives us knowledge, understanding, and discernment, helping us to recognize when to overlook and when to address offenses.

There are at least four excellent reasons to overlook an offense. First, you can often learn a great deal about another person or a situation when you overlook an "offense." It can give you understanding and power to look deeper into the reasoning behind the offense. Second, sometimes they didn't mean it; maybe they weren't thinking or didn't know their words or actions were offensive. Third, it's good to return the favor—meaning, how many times have we ourselves been offensive and thankfully, someone overlooked it? And fourth, just as is stated in the proverb, it gives you glory or in other words, it makes you look good. When you "look good" because you have patience and know how to appropriately overlook offenses, you become a more valuable leader.

I am thankful that we don't need to be born with a patient disposition but instead, we can acquire patience through pursuing wisdom. If we become wiser, then we will have more patience. It is also to God's glory when we are able to overlook an offense. It is through His rich, beautiful bounty of Proverbs, dedicated to obtaining wisdom, that we are given patience. Thank you, Lord!

"All Scripture is God-breathed and is useful for teaching, rebuking, correcting and training in righteousness, so that the servant of God may be thoroughly equipped for every good work" (2 Timothy 3:16-17).

Dear Jesus, thank You for what You did for us on the cross, for taking on all of our sins and all of our offenses. We want to serve You well. We want to win souls here on earth, so that others may know You and live eternally in Heaven. We ask You Lord, to help us to pursue wisdom that we may serve You to the best of our ability. All glory and honor to You, Lord Jesus Christ—always and forever, Amen.

Thoughts — Prayers — Doodles

A person's wisdom yields patience; it is to one's glory to **overlook an offense.**

Proverbs 19:11

Use Your Head!

*Ears that hear and eyes that see—
the LORD has made them both.
Proverbs 20:12*

One of the first exciting memories I have of growing up in the country is being accompanied by my dad and walking along a narrow, steep path through the woods to a fast-flowing river. As children we were never allowed to go down the path alone, so I rarely had the opportunity to see the muddy Maumee River. I loved it though. It evoked mystery and excitement.

When I was about six years old and my sister and cousin were around seven, we hatched a plot to walk down to the river . . . without an adult. I felt pressure to go along, but I was scared. I walked with them as far as the barn and then bailed out.

Why? Probably in part because I could hear my mother in my head saying, "God gave you eyes and ears—use 'em!" Often as a child I failed to "use my head" or "use my eyes and ears." I often failed to think things through and made some really stupid mistakes. If a person made a stupid mistake on the farm, it could be costly and sometimes deadly. Falling into the Maumee River as a child would have been deadly. Thankfully, my sister and cousin were fine, but they did get into some trouble for disobeying.

Using your ears to hear and your eyes to see will help keep you safe physically, emotionally, and spiritually.

We can be misled if we rely solely on what we hear, rather than what we hear *and* see. At times, we may *want* to believe something is true because it is less painful than facing the truth. The phrase "facing the truth" implies that previously we were not seeing clearly. Remembering this phrase can help us remember this proverb: eyes and ears are on the face, and both are helpful to discern truth.

Use your eyes and ears! Use your head! Think for yourself!

These sayings were drilled into my mind and they originated from the Proverbs. They helped keep me safe and steered me away from many dangerous mistakes. However, mistakes *can* be great teaching tools. In some ways, we probably learn more from our mistakes than our successes.

Being fearful of making mistakes can keep us from achieving the best that God has for us. If we surrender all of our learning—including our mistakes—to God, He will teach us through every situation.

Here's an awesome question that, when asked with a loving and safe attitude, can be a powerful teaching tool for children, "What's something that didn't go well today that you can learn from?" We can gain much wisdom if we focus on the learning that comes from the mistakes that we've made. And we can avoid many painful mistakes by using both our ears and our eyes.

We can learn from others' mistakes too. Thank God we don't have to make all of them on our own! We can avoid much pain by using our eyes and ears. This is what my mom was trying to drill into my mind, and I'm thankful for it.

Lord Jesus, life is very complicated at times, and understanding other people is often confusing to me. Help me to keep Your Word active in my mind and deeply memorized within my soul so that You may teach me through every situation. Help me Father, to keep my ears sensitive and my eyes opened. Help me to see and hear the way that You see and hear. I love You, Jesus, more than words can ever express. Thank you for teaching me daily. Amen.

Ears that **hear** and eyes that **see** — the **Lord** has made them both.

Proverbs 20:12

A New Plan

*There is no wisdom, no insight,
no plan that can succeed against the L*ORD.
Proverbs 21:30

I could feel God's hand upon my health coaching business. I named it after Him. It was called Eating Clean While Growing Closer to Christ and grew out of my business called Christ-centeredwellness.com. It was my plan to speak, teach, and coach Christian men and women across the United States to eat healthy and take good care of themselves through the power of the Holy Spirit and the teaching of His Word. I spent several years reading and studying in preparation. I earned certifications in nutrition and health coaching. I spent thousands of dollars so that I would be well equipped to help my brothers and sisters in Christ to eat healthy and hopefully live longer so that they could do kingdom work with more energy and more years.

It was a good plan. It was all coming together after five years of very hard work. It was successful and people's lives were being changed. Then my daughter died, leaving a beautiful, amazing little boy not yet four months old. Suddenly there was no time left for the plan. There was nothing more important than taking good care of her baby, who became my baby. And there is no one who can make my husband and me smile like he can.

Plans can slowly dissipate or suddenly end. They often fail due to a lack of discipline. But sometimes they fail because we have learned what God wanted us to learn through the venture, and perhaps He desires us to move forward with a new plan. We can rest in the knowledge that the plans God intends to succeed will succeed.

God gives wisdom. If we are seeking wisdom from God and asking for His help to make and implement a plan, we can trust that if it is God's will, it will succeed. If it is not God's will, it will not succeed. Period. His ways are not our ways. He sees all, knows all, and loves us completely. His way is perfect and He is to be trusted. If He has given us a new plan, then there is no shame in letting go of the old one. Of course, we must do the work necessary to help it succeed—that falls under "wisdom."

Having a plan fail can fuel distrust or even ignite fear. Fear is a powerful deterrent that the enemy uses to stop us from putting ourselves "out there" and trying something new. Lately, I have felt compelled to embrace fear . . . not the fear that the enemy throws my way, but rather the fear of the Lord. When the Battle of Indecision begins in my mind and Fear arises as the main character, I am aiming towards fearing the Lord above all things. This is no small feat. Reliance on memorized Scripture, prayer, and the leading of the Holy Spirit is crucial for success.

"The fear of the LORD is the beginning of wisdom" (Proverbs 9:10). If I fear disappointing God more than feeling embarrassed or feeling that I failed or anything else, then I am taking the hard steps towards wisdom. Walking through life accompanied by the wisdom of God is key to unlocking our true potential. He has designed each of us with unique giftings that we are to use to glorify God and further His kingdom. There is no safer place in the world than to be inside of God's ultimate plan. This is the journey God intends for each of us.

Dear Jesus, today and every day I desire to fear You above all things, to desire Your will above all else, to declare You as my greatest love. Please fill my heart with Your truth,

Your grace, Your wisdom, Your mercy, Your kindness, Your love, Your strength, and Your plan. Amen.

Thoughts — Prayers — Doodles

THERE IS NO WISDOM, NO INSIGHT, NO PLAN THAT CAN SUCCEED AGAINST THE Lord

PROVERBS 21:30

War Horse

*The horse is made ready for the day of battle,
but victory rests with the LORD.
Proverbs 21:31*

Warrior is the name of a famous war horse who showed tremendous courage, strength, and loyalty during World War I. He sometimes trembled underneath his rider's legs but continued to follow bravely and obey his commander. His courage influenced other horses to stand and fight.

This Proverb is about a horse, a battle, the Lord our Commander, and victory.

We, Christians, are the horses being "made ready" for the day of battle. The battle is life here on earth. We can *allow* ourselves to become trained "war horses" prepared to go into battle for our Commander—God. Life is the battle and victory is delivered through our Lord Jesus Christ. The horse that is being made ready is most valuable if she is obedient to her owner, her commander, her Lord.

A valuable war horse will listen and respond to her commander. She must learn to trust her commander. The commander must transfer the needed information so that the war horse can do a good job. Our commander gives us all the information we need through the Bible, prayer, and the Holy Spirit.

If it feels like a lot of battles have come your way in life, take heart. We have a trustworthy Commander who has given us the right information to win, even when it seems as though we have lost. We will learn what He wants us to learn in every battle of life that we fight *if* we continue to listen and trust our Commander. His promise is that He will never leave us.

We are being trained by the Holy Spirit and the Word of God to be wise. We are learning to be sensitive to the sound of the Holy Spirit and to quickly obey our God. This makes us effective to go into battles with our Commander the Lord. Our Savior does not want us going into battles alone. He wants to guide us. We need to listen to Him.

We are stronger for having won other battles in life. As we win more battles, we become more valuable on the front lines. This is a good thing—an honorable walk, an honorable journey, an honorable fight. We are confident because we know and trust our Commander. We trust our Lord because we have seen His Hand in the day of battle and He always wins in the end. "For the LORD your God is the one who goes with you to fight for you against your enemies to give you victory" (Deuteronomy 20:4).

The best war horse is sometimes made from the strongest, most obstinate and stubborn horse. If you have any of these qualities (like I do), there is hope! The Lord needs all of our hearts to train us to be ready for the day of battle. And remember . . . victory rests with the Lord. He has already won the battle. The question is whether we give Him all of our hearts, our unquestionable obedience, so that we may be used in the battle. I want to be used in the battle. I am a war horse. Are you?

Lord, I want so much to be used by you to further Your Kingdom. On this earth are many battles and I believe that You choose and train Your war horses. You are always with me. Help me to be alert to Your voice and immediately obey Your commands. Amen.

The horse is made ready for the day of battle, but victory rests with the Lord.

Proverbs 21:31

Don't Waste Your Time

Do not speak in the ears of a fool,
for he will despise the wisdom of your words.
Proverbs 23:9 (NET)

Can you imagine Jesus trying to convince a fool that He was right? Can you imagine Jesus repeating Himself with more passion and fervor to try and get His point across? I can't. Jesus calmly left it up to others as to whether they would hear the wisdom of His words. He often said, "Those who have ears, let them hear" (Matthew 11:15).

The proverb says not to speak to a fool. Why? Why does it matter if fools scorn the wisdom of your words? How does that affect you?

Imagine you are playing baseball and delivering beautiful perfect throws to another catcher. The catcher simply stares at you, arms hanging down, never attempting to catch the ball. With a sour look, the catcher mocks your efforts.

Can that take a toll on you? Absolutely. Eventually, you'll probably stop throwing the ball. Why bother? It doesn't make a difference if you throw it or not. But throwing the ball to a catcher who wants to become a better catcher is exciting and will add value to both of you.

Sharing wisdom with a fool can drain your energy and chip away at your confidence. The fool believes that your words are not worthy of interest. You will be mocked. You will be *despised*, which is a negative, shaming action intended to show disrespect or disapproval.

This proverbs states that it is important to protect yourself and to choose wisely when investing in other people. Offering wisdom to a fool is worthless, so save your energy. Save your effort. Invest in those who desire to learn.

Lord, Jesus, Your Word says that if we desire wisdom, we are to ask for it and You will give it to us. I desire wisdom now, Lord—in all that I say and do today—please give me Your supernatural Spirit to make wise decisions, to speak with wisdom, and to choose carefully with whom I share my words and my heart. Amen.

Thoughts — Prayers — Doodles

Do not speak in the ears of a fool,

for he will despise the wisdom of your words.

Proverbs 23:9

I Give You My Heart

*Apply your heart to instruction
and your ears to words of knowledge.*
Proverbs 23:12

In school, we were taught to apply our brains to gather information so that we would have knowledge.

This proverb says that to learn wisdom, we are to apply our hearts to instruction so that we would have knowledge. This is vastly different! He could have said, "Apply your mind to instruction," but no! It is your heart that Christ wants first. With your heart in His hands, He can do all that He wants to do in and through you. With your heart turned towards Christ and actively seeking instruction, it is going to be a better day . . . and over time, it is going to be a better life.

"Love the Lord your God with all your heart and with all your soul and with all your mind. This is the first and greatest commandment" (Matthew 22:37–38). Even in these words, Jesus mentions the heart first. We must never underestimate how precious our hearts are to God.

Applying our hearts to instruction means fully opening our hearts to the instruction of God our Father and expecting to see Him in our lives. We can expect him to be here in this moment and every moment of our day. We can listen and deliberately train our ears to be sensitive to His words of knowledge delivered through the Holy Spirit, who is sometimes amazingly subtle.

Attaining wisdom is not exclusive to the intelligent or the educated, and this Proverb shows how deliberately God evens out the playing field. A closed heart plus intelligence equals foolishness. A heart opened to God's instruction equals wisdom, regardless of one's intelligence or education. I love that.

Lord Jesus, You are my teacher, my Savior, and my friend. I treasure my relationship with You more than words can express and I desire to know more of Your wisdom. Help me to give my heart to You every moment of the day and keep my ears sensitive to hear Your truth. Amen.

Thoughts — Prayers — Doodles

Apply your heart to instruction and your ears to words of knowledge.

Proverbs 23:12

Listen

*Listen, my son, and be wise, and set your heart on the right path.
Do not join those who drink too much wine
or gorge themselves on meat,
for drunkards and gluttons become poor,
and drowsiness clothes them in rags.
Proverbs 23:19–21*

Whoa! There is so much information in these three verses. They belong together but it will help to break it up into two parts. The following devotion is part one. Look at verse 19 as if it were spaced like this:

Listen,

Listen, my son,

Listen, my son, and be wise,

Set your heart on the right path.

The first command is to *listen* . . . listen to the Holy Spirit, to Jesus Christ, to God our Father. Sensitize our ears, hearts, minds and souls so that we listen; so that we pause . . . and listen.

"Listen, *my son*." Let us *never* forget that we are sons and daughters of a King. God, the Creator of the Universe, Who is sitting on His throne in heaven calls us His children. He claims us as His sons and daughters. We belong to Him and in His family. We are not forgotten. We are loved, cared for, and listened to by the most powerful King in the world, now and forevermore.

And when we listen, we have the opportunity to "be wise." It is a choice that is given to us by our Heavenly Father because of His deep love for us. We must make the *choice* to "be wise."

"Set your heart on the right path." Why? Because it all starts and ends with our hearts. This gives all of us a fighting chance. If, in this moment, we surrender our hearts to God our Father through the power of the Holy Spirit, then our hearts are on the right path and we will not go astray no matter what. "Even there Your hand will guide me, Your right hand will hold me fast" (Psalm 139:10). If our hearts are on the right path, then our minds will follow, and our words and actions will be in alignment with God's will. Undeniably wise.

Listen,

Listen, my son,

Listen, my son, and be wise,

Set your heart on the right path.

Lord, Jesus, You know me and all of my insecurities, shortcomings, and foolish tendencies. Because of You and Your redemptive blood on the cross, You have given us power through Your Holy Spirit, to surrender our hearts to You; to pause, to listen, and to choose wisdom. Help me today, Father, to be a child who pleases You. Amen.

Thoughts — Prayers — Doodles

Listen, my son and be **wise**, and set your **heart** on the right path. Do not join those who drink too much wine or gorge themselves on meat...

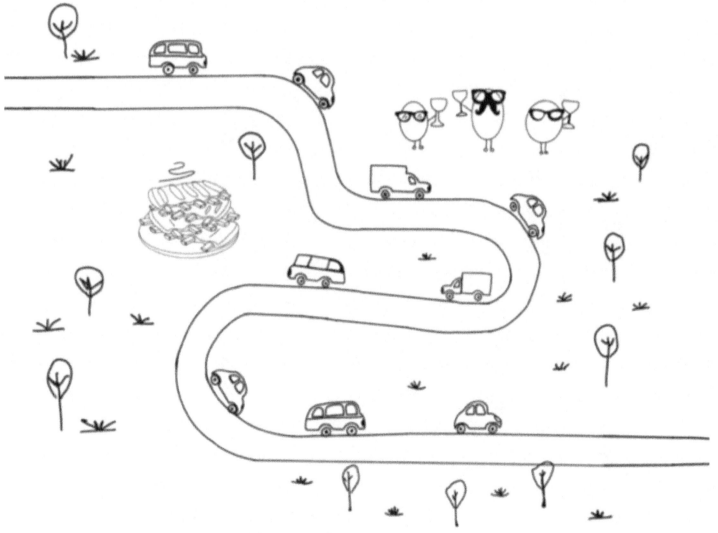

Proverbs 23:19-20

I Hate It When It Hurts!

Listen, my son, and be wise, and set your heart on the right path.
Do not join those who drink too much wine
or gorge themselves on meat,
for drunkards and gluttons become poor,
and drowsiness clothes them in rags.
Proverbs 23:19–21

Proverbs 23:19 talks about listening, remembering you are a child of God, being wise, and keeping your heart set on the right path. Verses 20 and 21 add to this: Do not join those who drink or eat too much because they will become poor and lazy and not have enough money to even clothe themselves well.

We know that drinking too much wine or alcohol is foolish. It can rob your ambition, cause depression; it is costly and impairs judgement. But the second part of the verse—gorging yourselves on meat and being gluttonous—I believe we often dismiss as less of a problem than this proverb declares. Wisdom is grouping these two things, drunkards and gluttons, together! Ouch, I hate it when it hurts!

Eating too much will cause our bodies to become sluggish, slow, drowsy, unproductive, depressed, and ill. It is typical of the pattern of sin. A futile promise followed by painful truth. The enemy can entice us by promising that we will feel better when we eat all of this or that. But "feeling good" lasts only a moment before truth registers in our spirit, body, and mind. Suddenly we know that we made our stomachs more important than taking care of our body—the temple where the Holy Spirit resides.

Recognizing that being drunk or gluttonous are both serious behaviors that take us off of the "right path" is wisdom expounded. Turning to the Holy Spirit the first thing in the morning and asking for His help in keeping us on the right path is the antidote. Keeping His Word in your heart and in your mind is wisdom. It is powerful.

Lord Jesus, it is You and You only that I want to focus on pleasing today. Please remind my heart that you go before me and that I can trust You in all things. Help me, Holy Spirit, to stay on the right path. Help me not to turn to alcohol or food or worry or anything else except You. You go before me on my journey in life and one day You will take me into heaven. Help me to keep my eyes fixed on You and rest in Your peace, always. Amen.

Thoughts — Prayers — Doodles

It's Not Easy

Eat honey my son, for it is good;
honey from the comb is sweet to your taste.
Know also that wisdom is like honey for you:
if you find it, there is a future hope for you,
and your hope will not be cut off.
Proverbs 24:13–14

Finding honey out in the wild is not easy. You must have a general idea of where to look and then search it out. When you find it, it is guarded by little insects that will sting you. They want to deter you from taking their honey. They value their honey with such ferocity that they are willing to die (by stinging you) to protect their treasure!

Finding wisdom is not easy either. We have to know where to find it. God included an entire book in the Bible called Proverbs dedicated to those who desire to pursue wisdom. We search for wisdom by reading, memorizing, and meditating on the Proverbs, just like we are doing now. What is trying to deter us from getting that wisdom? I like picturing the deterrents as little bees that I can swipe away. One is named "not enough time," another is named "lack of discipline," and another is named "you can't start another habit." I can shoo all of these away with the truth: God values wisdom. God values us. God desires that we pursue wisdom. To do this, we must make the effort, take the time, and establish the habit of seeking wisdom.

Proverbs says that if we find wisdom, there is a future hope for us and our hope will not be cut off. Hope is a powerful motivator. Sometimes the problems in our lives are very complex and heavy. Having wisdom as you navigate through the problems changes the outcome. It changes your life. It changes your perspective. It changes you.

Lord Jesus, Your wisdom is beautiful and complete and perfect. You lived a life here on earth as both fully human and fully God. The stories that You left us in the Bible are filled with wisdom. They are honey to our lips. Help us to learn from You and Your Word. Help us to discern the proverbs and parables that we may gain a heart of wisdom. Thank you and Amen.

Thoughts — Prayers — Doodles

Know also that
wisdom
is like honey for you:
if you find it,
there is a future hope
for you,
and your hope
will not be cut off.

Proverbs 24:14

Take Care of Yourself

*"Like a city whose walls are broken through
is a person who lacks self-control."*
Proverbs 25:28

Sometimes when I read Proverbs 25:28, I have to ward off a sense of inadequacy or guilt or anxiety. But today after I read it, God gave me a different perspective.

The wall protects the city. It is a boundary that keeps people in and danger out. The wall wasn't built in a day. It took time. It took practice to get it right. It took knowledge and experimentation as to how to build it and what materials were best to use. Sometimes the wall needed repair and special attention given to a particular area. Sometimes the wall fell apart when it wasn't maintained. When the wall broke down, it was dangerous. There were obvious visual and physical reasons to keep it in repair.

When people saw the wall maintained, they respected the value of what was inside, realizing it was worth being protected. If the wall was broken down, it could be assumed that the people inside had *lost their ability* to take care of the wall or *just didn't care enough* to take care of it—which would result in allowing danger to come through.

The wall is a boundary that protects the valuable city. The parallel here is that we must have boundaries to protect our hearts, minds, and bodies. God values our hearts, minds, and bodies as is evidenced when Jesus teaches the first and greatest commandment: "Love the Lord your God with all your heart and with all your soul and with all your mind. This is the first and greatest commandment" (Matthew 22:37—38).

We protect our *hearts* by inviting and allowing the Holy Spirit to reside there. This we do by prayer. We protect our *minds* by reading with faith the Bible and memorizing His Word. We protect our *bodies* by eating healthy and exercising. We are made up of spirit, mind, and body, which all have need of protection. We use our self-control to protect each of these areas.

Our hearts must be willing to be broken and built back up by the Holy Spirit. As followers of Jesus Christ, we are called to reach out to others—both Christians and non-Christians. We will be hurt in the process. Our walls will take hits and our hearts will be broken, but the leading of the Holy Spirit builds us back up, making us stronger and wiser.

Our minds will sometimes want to be swayed towards negativity and lies. Meditating day and night on the Word of God protects our minds by teaching us about God's infinite love for His people. Building a wall of truth in our minds is a powerful, game-changing way to live a life that honors God. It is the ultimate "mind-set."

Our bodies also require being built up. We are responsible to God for what we eat and drink and how we take care of our bodies. Christians can tend to turn away from this responsibility because it is difficult and, at times, frustrating. No one receives a perfect body or perfect health. We are responsible for the imperfect bodies that God has given us here on earth. We are to take care of them. "Therefore, I urge you, brothers and sisters, in view of God's mercy, to offer your bodies as a living sacrifice, holy and pleasing to God—this is your true and proper worship" (Romans 12:1).

Lord, Your Word says, "Like a city whose walls are broken down is a person who lacks self-control." I know that you value self-control and this is sometimes a struggle for me.

Please fill my heart with your Holy Spirit that I may become increasingly sensitive to Your Voice. Fill my mind with your memorized Word that I am more easily shaped to become like You. Help me to respect my body by eating right and exercising. Always and in all things, let me sing praise to You and give You all of the Glory! Amen!

Thoughts — Prayers — Doodles

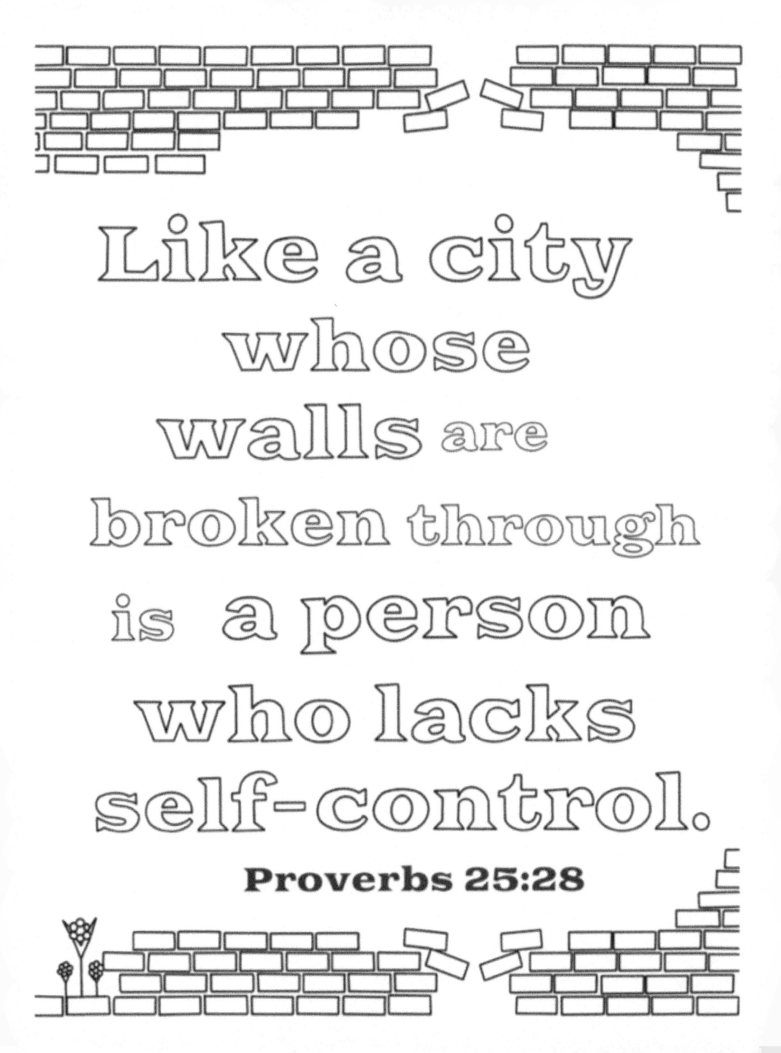

Humility is Key

Do you see a person wise in their own eyes?
There is more hope for a fool than for them.
Proverbs 26:12

If we think we are wise because of who we are, then even a fool is better off than us. All wisdom comes from God. "The fear of the LORD is the beginning of wisdom" (Proverbs 9:10).

The moment we start to believe that we are wise because of our own doing is the exact moment we discard humility and allow arrogance to occupy our spirit. God loves humility because it uncovers a teachable spirit.

Our wisdom depends on the Holy Spirit working and speaking through us, which depends on our hearts being opened that we may hear. What we hear depends on what we put into our hearts and minds.

There isn't another book in the Bible that informs the reader more clearly of its intent than the Book of Proverbs. "The proverbs of Solomon son of David, king of Israel: for attaining wisdom and discipline; for understanding words of insight" (Proverbs 1:1–2). Memorizing and studying these verses allows the Holy Spirit access to train us in wisdom.

We will never have it all down. The wise will never be wise 100 percent of the time. We will never "arrive" until we meet Jesus face to face. But if we study Proverbs today, meditating and memorizing verses, then we will be wiser today than we were yesterday.

We know that through our own flesh we are not wise, but with the Spirit of God working through us, wisdom is attainable. We give all glory to God and we depend on Him for wisdom. It is His to give and His to claim. We are servants working for the Most High, who loves us deeply, is forever faithful, and promises wisdom to those who seek it.

Lord Jesus, You are the ultimate teacher and You studied, memorized, and recited Scripture. Help us to memorize and meditate on Your Word today, Lord, that we may gain a heart of understanding; that we may gain more wisdom; and that we may win souls for the Kingdom of God. All glory always to You, heavenly Father. Amen.

Thoughts — Prayers — Doodles

> Do you see a person wise in their own eyes? There is more hope for a fool than for them.
>
> Proverbs 26:12

Faceless Facebook Fraught with Problems

*Like one who grabs a dog by the ears
is a passerby who meddles in a quarrel not his own.
Proverbs 26:17 (Berean Study Bible)*

My grandma was under five feet tall, but she packed a lot of wisdom into her small frame. I often heard her say, "You just need to mind your own business." It was more than a statement; it was an expectation of behavior.

In this age of social media, minding your own business seems about as easy as grasping oil with the hand. Before social media, we looked each other in the eye as we held conversations, discussions, and disagreements. Before we post or respond to someone on social media, it would be wise to picture the person(s) to whom we are talking and to show the love of Jesus Christ. If we could see the person, we might notice her face expressing humor, stress, dismay, humility, or other emotions. It's too easy to absorb a post at face value . . . without seeing the face, even though it's "*Face*book." Just because we cannot physically see the person, we should never discount his or her spiritual value. Being "faceless" on Facebook is fraught with problems.

Thankfully, we are spiritual beings and prayer reaches past computers and the walls of a home. Wisdom and discernment reveal when we should or should not voice our opinions. In the end, teaching others about Jesus Christ is more important than any political situation or quarrelsome topic. As ambassadors for Christ, we will be more effective if we pray before posting, listen before leading, and love with the love of Jesus Christ, always.

Lord Jesus, we are living in strange times and none of this catches You by surprise. Please give us wisdom and discernment so that we can share the truth of the gospel and the love of who You are with others. Help us remember that we are all spiritual beings who are desperate to feel Your love, whether we recognize our need for You or not. There is a right time to speak up and a right time to let things go, but it is always the right time to see others with the love of Jesus Christ. We are thankful to be Your ambassadors, Lord Jesus. Amen.

Thoughts — Prayers — Doodles

Like one who grabs a dog by the ears is a passerby who meddles in a quarrel not his own.

Proverbs 26:17

There's a Price

The prudent see danger and take refuge,
but the simple keep going and pay the penalty.
Proverb 27:12

An old woman in an Alaskan Inuit Village told this story: Two young boys had been standing at the top of a hill talking about sliding down the snowy slope. A small frozen lake was at the base of the hill. All of a sudden one of the boys took off and quickly slid down the hill. The snow-covered lake was not completely frozen, and he went under the ice and tragically did not come back up.

The old woman sadly recounted, "It's always the young and fast ones who die first."

In order to see danger, we must be *prudent*—meaning our thoughts and actions are governed by reason. We can use wise reasoning to decide how to spend and save our money, how to protect our closest relationships, how to navigate through dangerous situations, how to spend our time, how to make good business decisions, and how to work with difficult people.

By looking down the hill, up the road, and around the corner . . . looking past what is directly in front of us, we are better equipped to see where danger resides. Using reason, discipline, and prayer gives us wisdom and guides us away from disaster and towards safety. It also shows us when there is no danger. It helps us not to waste time over needless or irrational fears. Prudence means we know when to pull back and when to move forward, when to save and when to spend, when to protect and when to trust.

If we don't learn to see danger and take refuge, we will be foolish and pay a penalty. It can even be deadly to see danger and ignore taking refuge. This is foolishness. Both wisdom and foolishness have a price.

Lord Jesus, there are so many things that we do not know and there are wildly dangerous roads in life. We are thankful to serve the God who sees and knows everything. You promise to give us wisdom if we cry aloud for it. We cry aloud now for Your wisdom, Lord. Help us to have prudence in what we say and do so that we can honor You with our resources, time, and relationships. All glory to You, God Almighty, both now and forever more. Amen.

Thoughts — Prayers — Doodles

The prudent **see** danger and take **refuge,** but the simple keep going and pay the penalty.

Proverbs 27:12

Lead Well . . . Follow Well

*When a country is rebellious, it has many rulers,
but a man of discernment and knowledge maintains order.
Proverbs 28:2*

There are two sides to this Proverb: the responsibility of the leader and the responsibility of those being led. We are ambassadors for Christ and held to standards determined by God.

Although I have never been in charge of a country, this proverb applies to all who are in leadership. Whether you are running a Bible study, a business, a home, or a country, it is necessary to maintain order. Maintaining order is accomplished by having discernment, understanding, knowledge, and wisdom.

Understanding the people, the structure of the organization, and the organization's goals and values provides leaders with necessary knowledge and helps them to maintain order.

It is the leaders' job to be assertive if they feel that their leadership role is being usurped. It is common to have people in a class or study who believe they should be in charge rather than the appointed leader. It is your job as a leader to respectfully, kindly, and assertively maintain order and work towards accomplishing the established goals. Those who are following are counting on you to lead them.

Not everyone will agree with you or maybe even like you, but if you are called by God to be the leader, then you accept that as part of the job.

If you are a teacher or a coach or a boss, you may have the luxury to expect respect from your people. This is the way it used to be in the United States. Respect for leaders was a matter of manners and good upbringing. In the 1960s and '70s it became popular for the youth to wear ripped jeans and old t-shirts. I remember my grandmother chastising me as a teenager when I would dress this way. She found it disrespectful and asked me with genuine curiosity, "Why don't you dress nicer? Why, every day I dress as if I were going to meet the President of the United States!" Every day she took great care in how she dressed so that even if she met the most important leader in the United States, she would look respectful. She didn't differentiate between whether the president was a Democrat or a Republican. The office of the president of the United States deserved her respect because the president was the leader. Respect is communicated in the way that we dress, the way that we act, and the way that we talk. Respect for our leaders is a godly concept that I believe many Christians find easy to throw aside. As Christians, whether we have a Democratic president or a Republican president, we are called to bring our thoughts and words captive to Christ. "If anyone speaks, he should do it as one speaking the very words of God" (1 Peter 4:11).

Lord Jesus, You are the ultimate teacher and leader. You lead us perfectly and You follow God the Father perfectly. Lord, help me to lead well and follow well. Help me to listen carefully to Your Holy Spirit and let it guide my thoughts, my words, my actions, and my life. Lord, please help me to please You in all that I say and do. Amen.

Thoughts — Prayers — Doodles

When a country is rebellious, it has many rulers, but a man of discernment and knowledge maintains order.

Proverbs 28:2

I've Got You

*Those who trust in themselves are fools,
but those who walk in wisdom are kept safe.
Proverbs 28:26*

On my shelf is an unimpressive-looking landscape picture of a barren dessert. It is precious to me. I took the photo while on top of a small mountain in Botswana moments before I was to speak for the very first time about Proverbs. I was nervous. A large group of worship leaders and pastors from Africa was assembled and ready to listen.

The weight of effectively communicating the Word of God was heavy on my shoulders and I felt inadequate, so I went to the mountain alone to pray. Quite suddenly, the Lord impressed this upon my heart, "Don't worry. I've got you. I've got this." A smile replaced my worried face. I took the picture because I wanted to visually remember the moment. The landscape was unimpressive, but the power of God was all over that view.

When I go to pick up my baby from the crib and he is fussing, I say to him, "Don't worry. I've got you. I've got you," and he quiets. We are not alone and we are not so different from a little baby. We need guidance, love, support, and arms around us to continue to do the work God has called us to do. We need to trust that God "has us" and He has our work in His hands.

It would be foolish for me to believe that I can effectively speak about Proverbs without trusting God and asking Him for wisdom. It is foolish for us to believe that we can do His kingdom work without trusting Him and asking Him for wisdom. I believe He wants us to remember, "Don't worry, I've got you. I've got this."

Lord Jesus, You are the greatest communicator that has ever walked this earth. You taught us perfectly and Your word is filled with power. Help us, Jesus, to remember to actively put our trust in You and to ask You for wisdom. I am so thankful to be a servant to the One who sacrificially has me in His arms. Help me to remember Your character, Your faithfulness, and Your love that reaches beyond the heavens. You are my God and my Savior and I can picture You saying, "I've got you. I've got this." Thank you, Jesus. I love you.

Thoughts — Prayers — Doodles

Listen to Learn

Whoever remains stiff-necked after many rebukes
will suddenly be destroyed—without remedy.
Proverbs 29:1

So harsh! Without remedy? Without a cure? Without help? Not me! Surely, not me! Or, could it be?

My closest friends and family members have repeatedly told me that I am too busy. They have done this in the nicest of ways . . . and I have heard their advice, but it can be pretty easy for me to bat their wisdom aside. That would be stupid of me and, frankly, it could destroy me without remedy. Being too busy could destroy my health, my closest relationships, and my ability to teach and encourage others in their walk with Christ. Today I wrote down nine things that will help to keep me healthy and that will help me speak, teach, and encourage from a place of peace and good health. What's on your list? Here is mine:

Quiet Time with God every morning (this is a non-negotiable)

Preparing healthy foods and water for the day

Worshiping God through music

Exercising

Dates with my husband

Taking time to talk with friends and family

Walking in the woods

Art

Sticking with a nighttime routine and prioritizing sleep

What does the Holy Spirit want you to hear? Is there a place where you have been stiff-necked? God leads you with love. His Word also issues warnings to protect you. Being destroyed without remedy is harsh, and God's Word says it that way for a reason. We must listen to the Holy Spirit and change course if necessary.

Lord Jesus, we know that we can trust you with everything: with our lives, our families, our health, our time. Help us to listen to you and not be stubborn. Help us to continue to be a part of creating a better us rather than ignoring warnings that will hurt us. "There is a river whose streams make glad the city of God, the Holy Place where the Most High dwells. God is within her and she will not fall; God will help her at break of day" (Psalm 46:4–5). Fill us up, Lord, with your Holy Spirit, with Your Holy Water. We love You and trust You. Amen.

Thoughts — Prayers — Doodles

Whoever remains stiff-necked after many rebukes will suddenly be destroyed— without remedy.

Proverbs 29:1

A Nourished Soul

She gets up while it is still dark;
she provides food for her family and portions for her servant girls.
Proverbs 31:15

She gets up while it is still dark—the wise woman plans and provides what is important for her family and others who depend on her. She provides food that nourishes her family, but that isn't the only food necessary to thrive. The most important food is the Word of God, and it is crucial that the wise woman feeds herself *before* she takes care of others.

Getting up early and spending time with Jesus, in prayer, in Bible reading, and in praising Him through song, changes our perspective to be more like that of Jesus Christ. It will be the most important time spent in our day, but we *must plan* that time into our day. Jesus loves relationships and wants us to be close to Him. Getting up while it is still dark, grabbing our cup of coffee or tea, and having that quiet time honors Jesus. He is delighted that we take time to be with Him, listening to Him, talking with Him, praising Him, and remembering the deeds He has already done for us. God is always good and life is always unpredictable. We never know what a day may hold, but starting our day knowing that the God of the universe has us in his right hand gives us reassurance, power, and strength that will see us through even the most difficult of circumstances.

If Jesus is my best friend, the only one to completely understand me and to fully know what is best for me, . . . if He is willing to forgive all of my sins and to offer me a clean heart daily, . . . if He offers supreme wisdom and guidance, power, and strength, why would I ignore His desire for me to spend time with Him? I love Jesus. I need Jesus. I want Jesus. I want to know and understand

Him better, to be able to hear from Him more often and with better clarity. Close relationships don't just happen, they must be built, forged, tested, and honored.

Dear Jesus, You know me better than I will ever know myself and You love me more than anyone. Please help me to honor You by daily setting aside time to be with You. Help me to begin each day with my Bible, prayer, and a quiet heart ready to listen. You are the most important and influential person to me . . . fully human and fully God. Please help me to listen carefully to You in my quiet time and throughout my day. Amen.

Thoughts — Prayers — Doodles

She gets up while it is still dark; she provides food for her family and portions for her servant girls.

Proverbs 31:15

Acknowledgments

Writing this book and getting it into your hands has only been accomplished through amazing teamwork.

First, I thank Jesus Christ for saving me, loving me, and leading me to and through this writing endeavor. All glory and honor to You, my Savior, always.

Second, I thank my teammate for life, my husband, Kevin. I am so grateful to have you as my husband and I thank God that you asked me on a date thirty plus years ago. I love you.

Thank you to my sons, Lorenzo and Davinci. You inspire me to be a better person because you are both so very precious to me. Keep turning back to the Bible and perhaps especially to Proverbs—you'll need wisdom to navigate through this world. Thank you to my daughter, Claire. You taught me more about how to love than anyone on this earth. I'll always love you and I will hug you in heaven one day. Thank you to Olivia, my special niece. I look forward to seeing how your life unfolds. Stay close to Jesus – He loves you so much.

I am blessed to have had an amazing editor, Emily Varner. Thank you for being clear, sensitive, thorough, timely, and encouraging.

If you would like to stay in contact or receive a free Guide to Preparing Your Quiet Space, please visit Christ-centeredwellness.com. And, if you're interested in joining the Book Launch Team – we need you and would LOVE to have you! Please look on my website to see what's required and what you'll receive!

Finally, with extraordinary appreciation and gratitude, I thank the following people who have encouraged me, given me advice, proof-read early drafts, inspired me, shared my book with others, baby-sat while I wrote, and prayed for me.

Theresa Mobley
Charlie Roberts
Marianne Ferguson
Kathy Mobley
Chuck Mobley
Bev & Dennis Provagna
Mariah Rodriguez
Dwayne Moore
Sonia Moore
Dawn Kelley
Julie Myers
Marcia Peters
Derek Murphy
Emily Varner
Abby Loucks
Autumn Benson
Tina Seabolt
Lucy Muteneka
Rose Jabani
Ramona Bock
Paul Bock
TheChristianKristen (etsy)
The International Ladies' Proverbs Bible Study

You will never know how much I appreciate you and your willingness to help get this book into reader's hands. Thank you.
Suzanne

ABOUT THE AUTHOR

Hello Dear Reader,

It would make my day if I could take a walk with you and hear some of the stories of your life, maybe how God has intervened and put you back on the right path . . . His path. Maybe this book is even a part of that story—it certainly is a big part of mine.

Some time ago, I realized that my life would very likely not be getting any easier in the near future and that my best hope was to become wiser. I made the conscious decision to pursue wisdom and began reading a chapter of Proverbs each day. Years went by and I began writing personal stories that reflected the lessons of the Proverbs. Those writings became **Better, Stronger, Wiser.**

Asking for help has never been something that I do very well, but I do need your help. In order for this book (and other books yet to be written) to get into reader's hands, Amazon must receive many, many reviews. Would you please jump over to Amazon and leave an honest review? It can be just a couple of words (or more) and as many stars as you feel it deserves. To leave a review from your Amazon account, just click in upper right side of screen under "Returns & Orders", then find **Better, Stronger, Wiser** *and click on the yellow script saying "Ratings". That will open the reviews and there you can leave your own review by scrolling down on the left side and seeing where it says, "Write a Customer Review". Click on that button and you'll know what to do next. This process can take less than five minutes and will do wonders for helping me to continue to write. Thank you.*

I am very thankful for each person reading this book and would love to hear from you. Please feel free to email me with comments or suggestions. suzanneprovagna@gmail.com I would love to give you a few free gifts to help you on your journey of Christ-centered living. Please visit my website to receive them. www.christ-centeredwellness.com

It is my prayer that these stories inspire you to pursue wisdom by studying the Proverbs.

With gratitude and love,
Suzanne

Made in the USA
Columbia, SC
06 October 2023

24041351R00076